GIFTS

I Almost Got You

TO: ______________________________

FROM: ______________________________

DATE: ______________________________

GIFTS

I ALMOST GOT YOU

101 Great Gift Ideas and Perfect Excuses Why You Didn't Get Them

by

Dusty Rumsey

PUSH PULL PRESS

An imprint of JSA Publications, Inc.

Thanks are due the following:
Joseph S. Ajlouny for his support and encouragement, June I. Parker for her excellent services, Joe and Jeff at Brashayko Associates, Marilyn Krol, Jacqui Elliott, Rhodes and Sheila Rumsey, Shay Ramsey and Betsy Moore.

PUSH PULL PRESS

Published by Push/Pull/Press
an imprint of JSA Publications, Inc.
P.O.Box 37175,Oak Park, MI 48237 U.S.A.
Printed in the United States of America
2 3 4 5 6 7 8 9 0
ISBN: 0-929957-06-7
Library of Congress Catalog Number: 92-80468

To

Donna & Chandler

with love

I almost got you a coupon for a professional massage . . .

. . . But I used it myself—and do I feel great!

I almost got you an all expenses paid trip around the world . . .

. . . But then I remembered you only have two weeks vacation time.

I almost got you one free use of my credit card . . .

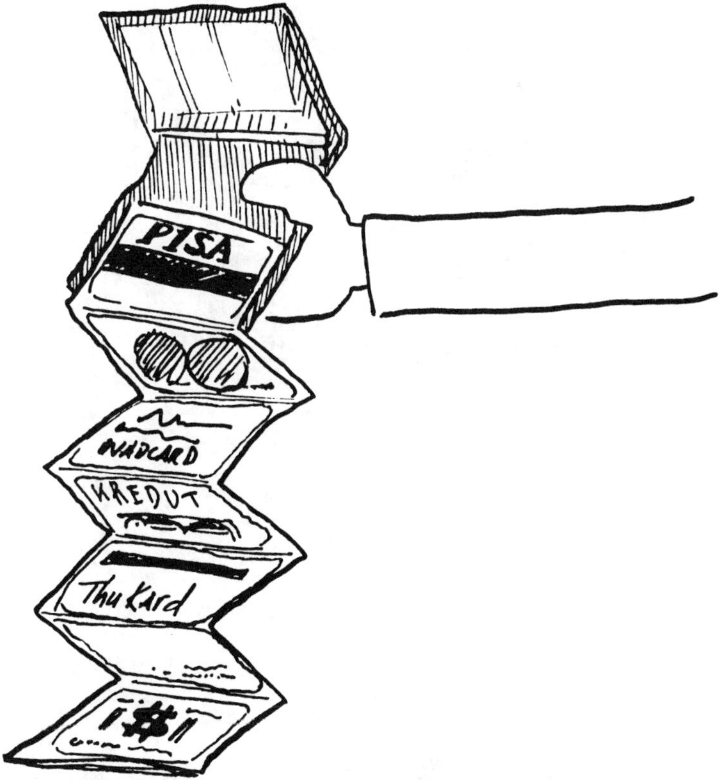

. . . But I'm over my limit, on all of them.

I almost got you a big screen TV . . .

. . . But I wouldn't want to turn your living room into a sports bar.

I almost got you a Lear Jet . . .

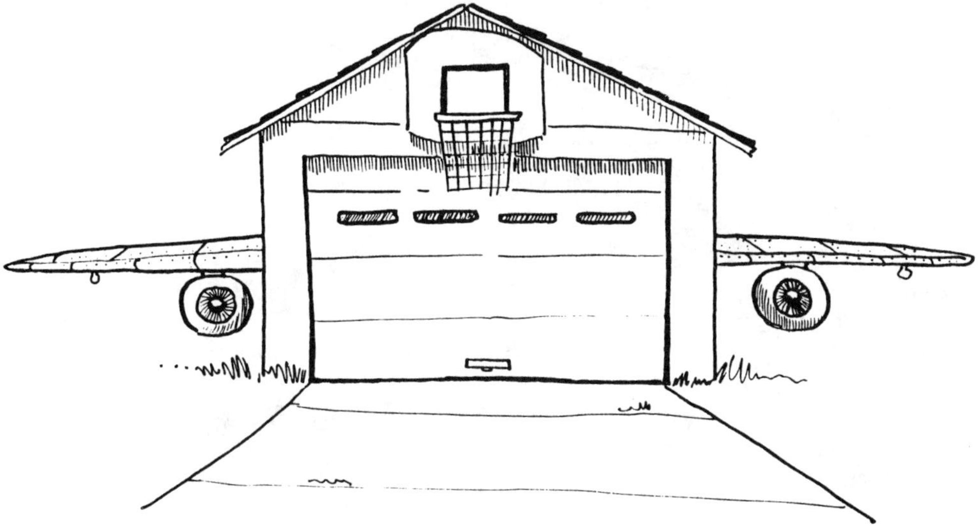

. . . But it wouldn't have fit in your garage without alterations.

I almost got you a full-length mink coat . . .

, , , But I figured I'd spare you the wrath of animal rights activists.

I almost got you this enormous diamond ring ...

. . . But it was so big it would have strained your arm.

I almost got you a week's vacation to Cancun. . .

. . . But it's the rainy season, and I can't get away now anyway.

I almost got you a new set of golf clubs . . .

. . . But what you really need is one good unbreakable club.

I almost got you a ship in a bottle kit . . .

. . . But I figured you'd rather have a bottle in a ship.

I almost got you a rare alligator wallet . . .

. . . But no matter how hard I fought, that alligator just wouldn't give it up !

I almost got you a limited edition, engraved swiss army knife . . .

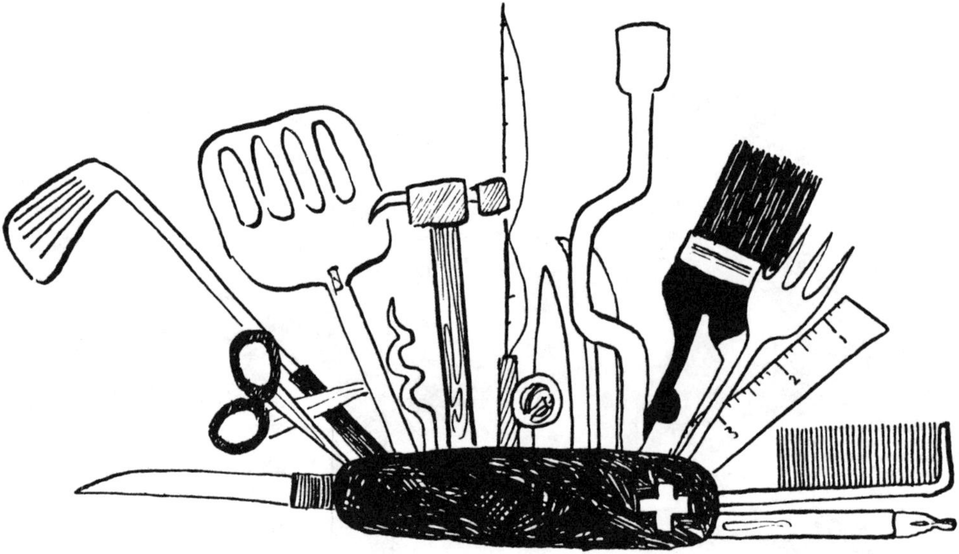

. . . But it dawned on me—you've already got most of those utensils in your kitchen.

I almost got you this adorable puppy . . .

. . . But then you'd need a bowl, a doghouse, food, collars, leashes, vaccinations—when you add it up, I just saved you a bundle.

I almost got you a great compact disc player . . .

. . . But what would you do with your huge record collection?

I almost got you a new VCR . . .

. . . But then you'd be burdened with choosing from millions of movies at the video store each visit.

I almost got you a cellular phone . . .

. . . But let's work on walking and chewing gum before you tackle driving and talking at the same time.

I almost got you a putting machine . . .

. . . But with your golf game, you'd need driving and chipping machines too.

I almost got you a rare bearskin rug . . .

. . . But I couldn't find any bears willing to part with one.

I almost got you a beautiful Rolex watch. . .

. . . But the little defective claw kept grabbing smiley face keychains.

I almost got you a great sailboat . . .

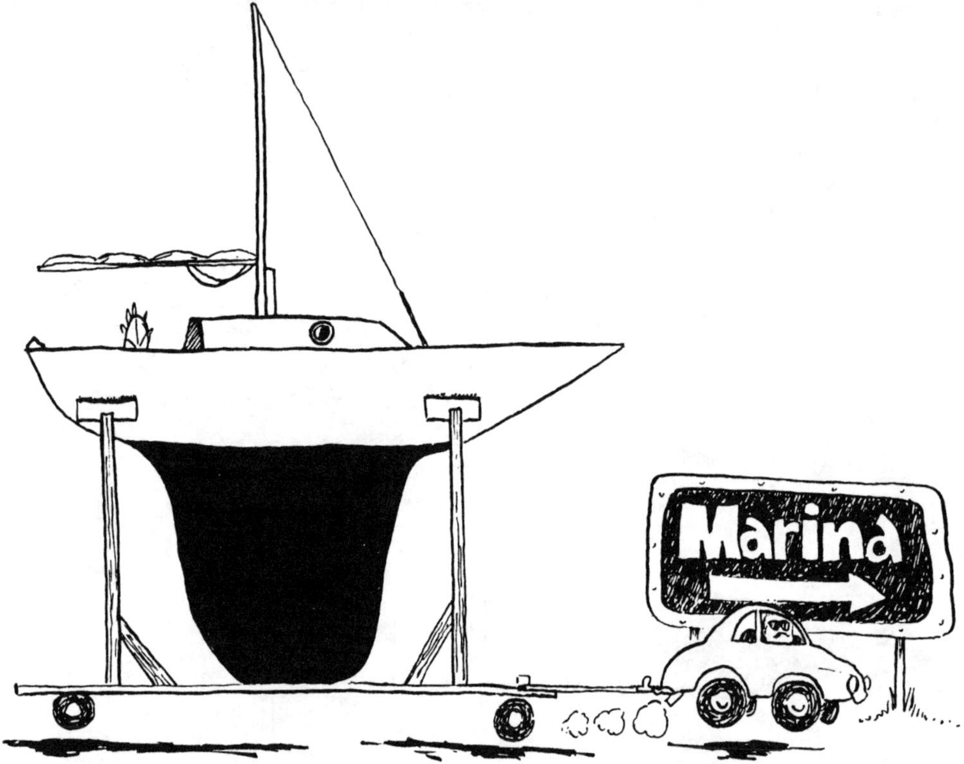

. . . But then I thought, they're such a pain to keep up, and your car is too small to tow it.

I almost got you a fine bottle of bourbon . . .

. . . Wait, maybe I did, hick!

I almost got you an excellent pair of skis . . .

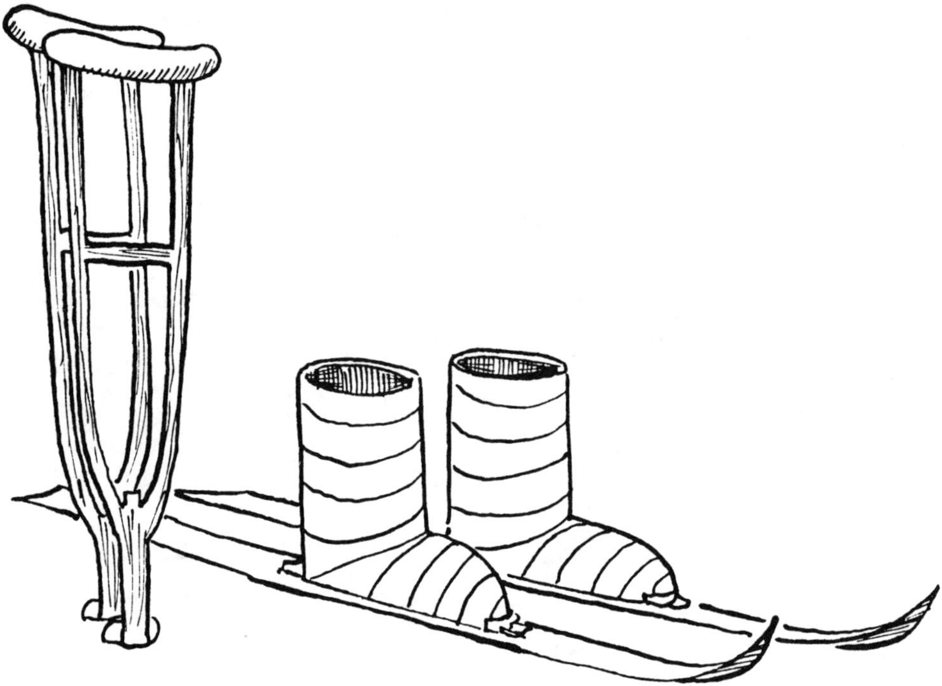

. . . But if you ever fell and broke you leg, I'd never forgive myself.

I almost got you a slick new Ferrari sportscar . . .

. . . But you're the one who preaches "Buy American," remember ?

I almost got you a camcorder . . .

. . . But then everybody would bug you to "Video" them.

I almost got you a skywritten message . . .

. . . But that pollutes the air, we have to think of the environment!

I almost got you an authentic rope hammock . . .

. . . But I couldn't find an insurance policy to go with it.

I almost got you a romantic serenade from a violinist . . .

. . . But he only knew one song—"Roll Over Beethoven".

I almost got you a Caribbean cruise . . .

. . . But I didn't think you'd enjoy being seasick for two weeks straight.

I almost got you a home IQ test . . .

. . . But I didn't want to depress you.

I almost got you a swimming pool . . .

. . . But you don't have anywhere to put it.

I almost got you a pony . . .

. . . But I checked and you can't have your yard zoned as a farm. Sorry.

I almost got you a genuine ten gallon hat . . .

. . . But then I remembered you've only got a five gallon head.

I almost got you an exer-cycle . . .

. . . But it's taken you years to develop the physique you've got.

I almost got you a new Rolls Royce . . .

. . . But I decided to save you the high cost of insurance.

I almost got you a stadium sky suite . . .

. . . But the only ones left are so high up you might've strained your eyesight.

I almost got you your own secluded Island . . .

. . . But I couldn't find anybody to gift wrap it.

I almost got you a riding lawnmower . . .

. . . But the waiting list for one with power steering is incredible.

I almost got you 50 yard line seats at the Super Bowl . . .

. . . But you can see the game so much better on television.

I almost got you a helicopter . . .

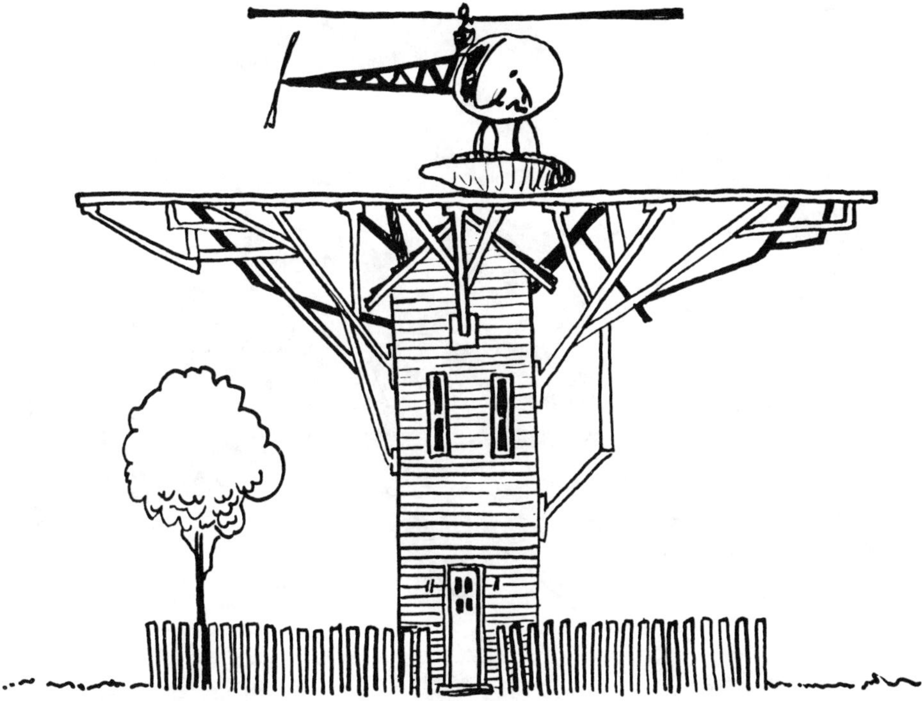

. . . But a helipad would've hurt your property value.

I almost got you tickets to the opera . . .

. . . But I want to keep you as a friend.

I almost got you a deluxe set of tools . . .

. . . But I remembered what happened the last time you "fixed" something.

I almost got you a bottle of imported French champagne . . .

. . . But did you know thousands are injured every year by high velocity corks?

I almost got you a fancy telescope . . .

. . . But your neighbors are hardly peeping tom material.

I almost got you a set of bathroom scales with digital read out . . .

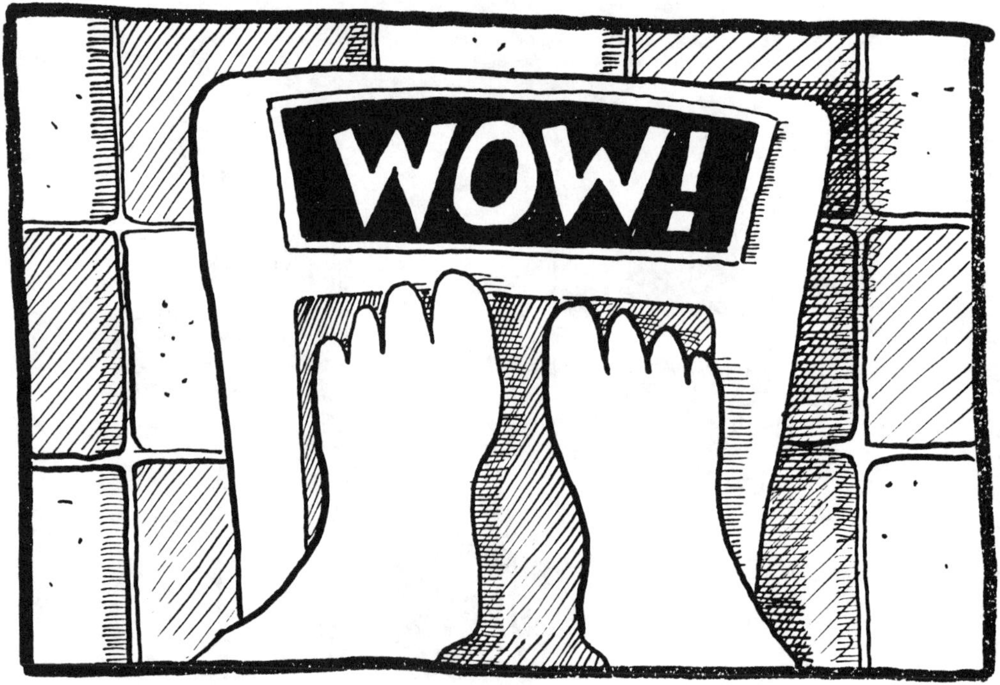

. . . But they're always *accurate*.. What a cruel gift.

I almost got you the latest Joy of Sex manual . . .

. . . But that would ruin the spontaneity.

I almost got you a bowling ball . . .

. . . But you spend plenty of time in the gutter without one.

I almost got you a nifty weedeater . . .

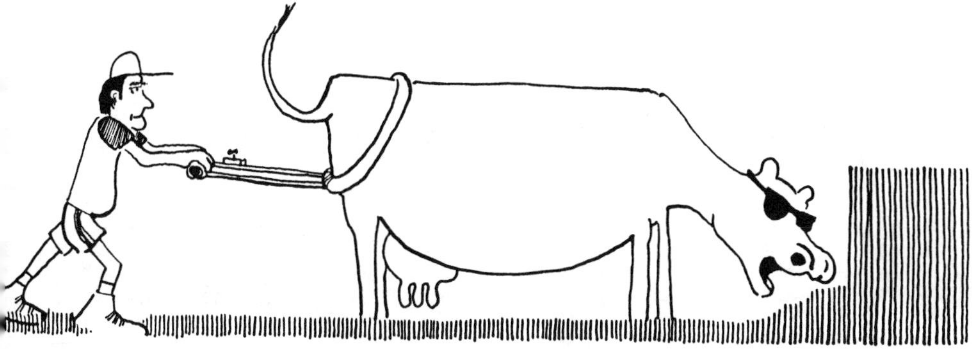

. . . But with your yard, what you really need is a cow.

I almost got you a gold cigarette lighter . . .

. . . But I'm going to wait until next year and get you a solid gold iron lung.

I almost got you a Strip—O—Gram . . .

. . . But the guy on the phone said your sister was busy.

I almost got you a gigantic jammin' boom box . . .

. . . But I didn't want to give your neighbors another reason to avoid you.

I almost got you a 99 function calculator . . .

. . . But that's 98 more functions than you know what to do with.

I almost got you a pair of sunglasses to make you look cool . . .

. . . But you'd need to ware them all over your body.

I almost got you a selection of coffees from around the world . . .

. . . But I haven't been around the world lately.

I almost got you a phone answering machine . . .

. . . But I didn't want to remind you that no one calls.

I almost got you a set of crystal goblets . . .

. . . But they'd break so easily during drinking games.

I almost got you a charm bracelet . . .

. . . But in your case, a bracelet isn't much help.

I almost got you a fancy pen set for your desk . . .

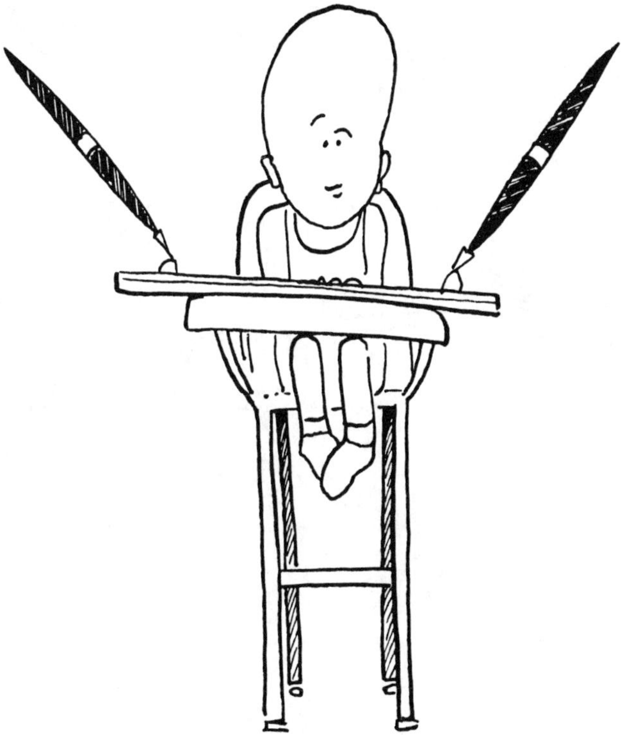

. . . But crayons are more your style.

I almost got you a bottle of mouthwash . . .

. . . But they were out of industrial strength formula.

I almost got you a box of hand-rolled Cuban cigars. . .

. . . But I had to use them as bribes in customs.

I almost got you a great Italian cook book . . .

. . . But you love TV dinners so much you think you're in show business.

I almost got you a pair of rollerblades . . .

. . . But they don't come in left-footed pairs.

I almost got you a stretch Limo for the evening . . .

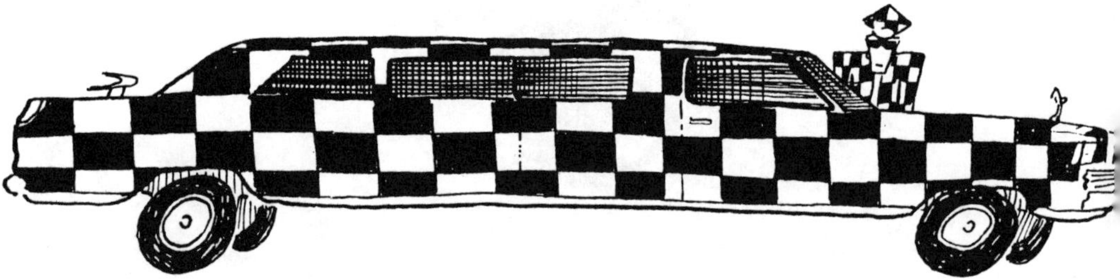

. . . But I couldn't decide between black or white.

I almost got you tickets to Wrestlemania . . .

. . . But I know how nervous you'd get watching your inlaws in the ring.

I almost got you some monogrammed hankies . . .

. . . But your initials aren't particularly flattering.

I almost got you reservations at a fancy restaurant . . .

. . . But they'd have reservations about letting you in.

I almost got you a priceless painting . . .

. . .But it had a price alright.
Boy did it have a price.

I almost got you a great Audio-Video entertainment center . . .

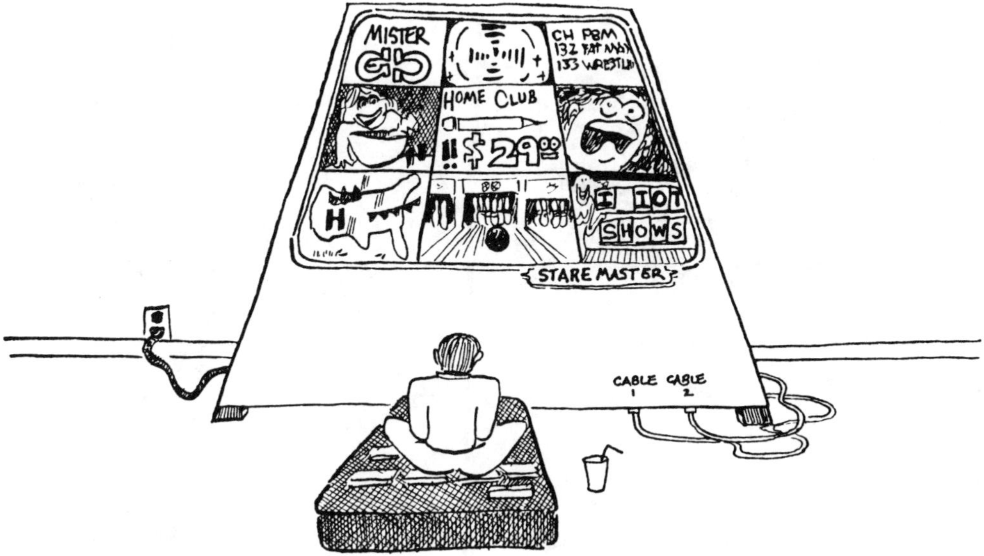

. . . But they only had one left so I bought it for myself. Sorry.

I almost got you an authentic black forest Cuckoo clock . . .

. . . But it would have driven your cat insane.

I almost got you a pair of expensive aviator glasses . . .

. . . But you don't exactly have a pilot's license.

I almost got you a set of darts . . .

. . . But you're such a poor sport, it could get dangerous !

I almost got you a holiday fruitcake . . .

. . . But I'd hate to destroy years of dental work.

I almost got you a box of chocolates . . .

. . . But I didn't want to dredge up memories of that terrible case of acne you had as a teenager.

I almost got you a hot air balloon ride . . .

. . . But you're afraid of heights, aren't you?

I almost got you a really fancy 10-speed touring bike . . .

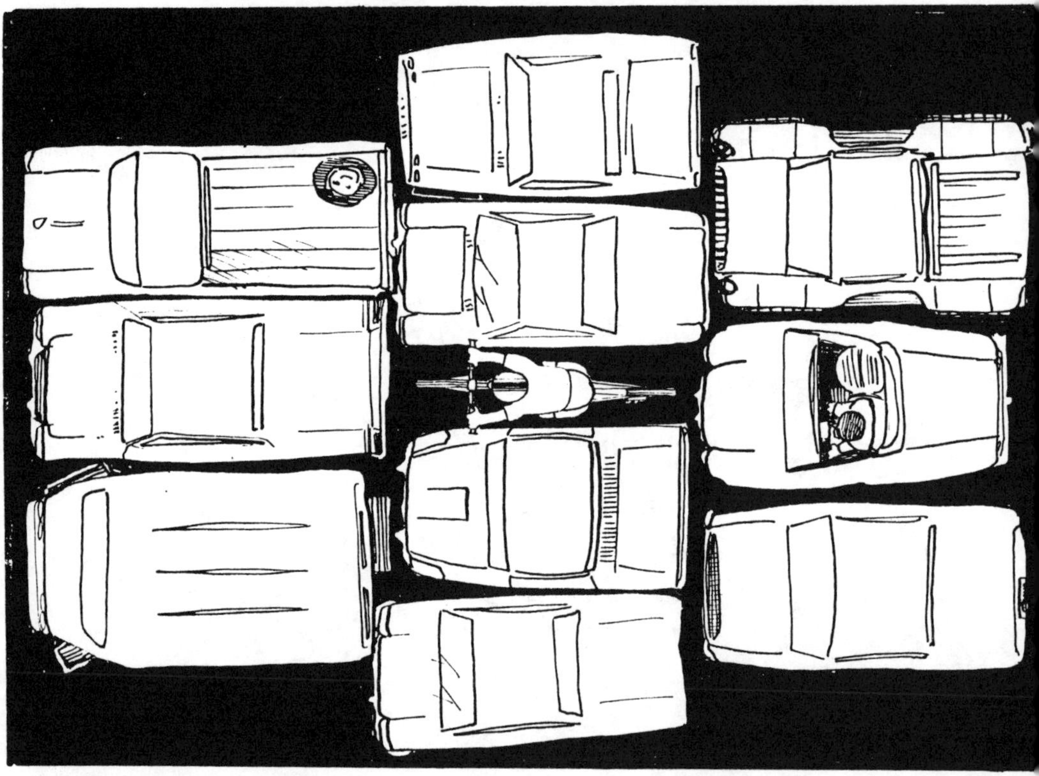

. . . But there's nowhere safe to ride anymore.

I almost got you a wad of cash . . .

. . . But the automated teller kept my card.

I almost got you some fur-lined underwear . . .

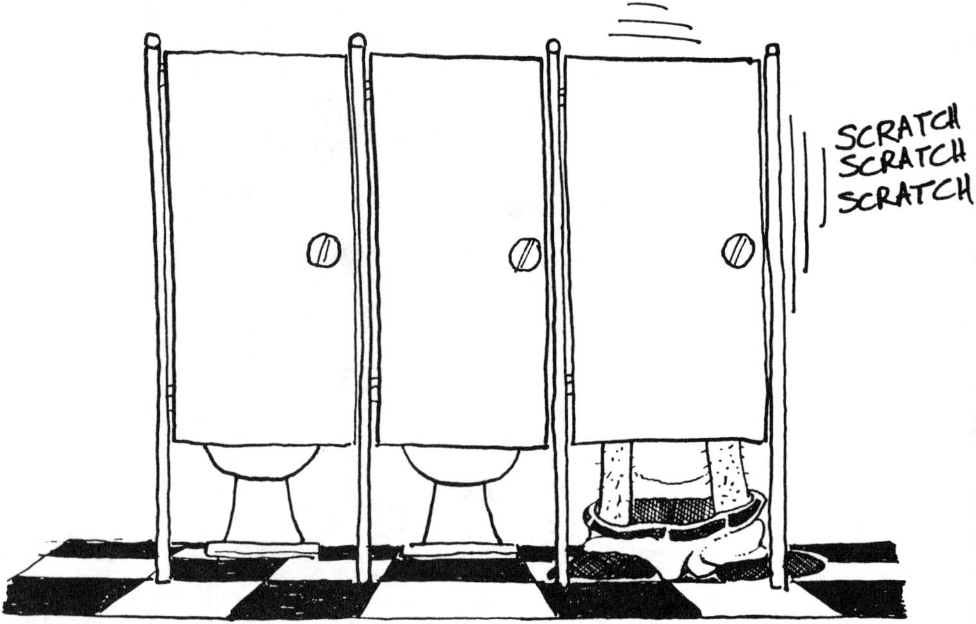

. . . But your allegies would—well—you get the picture.

I almost got you a paint by number kit . . .

. . . But its so hard to paint and count on your fingers at the same time.

I almost got you the complete works of William Shakespeare . . .

. . . But you think Macbeth is a fast food item.

I almost got you this beautiful coffee table book . . .

. . . But you see one coffee table, you've seen 'em all.

I almost got you a table at Chippendale's . . .

. . . But I don't want to be an accomplice to a potential assault charge.

I almost got you a tracing of your entire family tree . . .

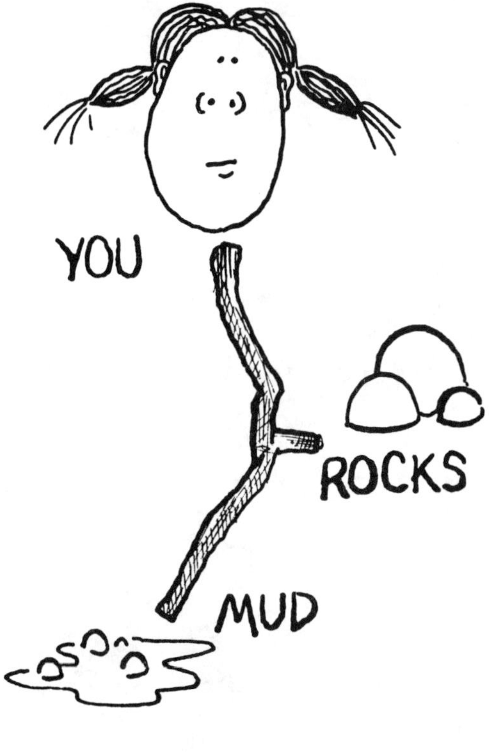

. . . But it turned out to be more like a twig.

I almost got you a pearl necklace . . .

. . . But I kept running out of breath.

I almost got you a snazzy new pair of sneakers . . .

. . . But I didn't know what type you need.

I almost got you a visit to see a fortune teller . . .

. . . But your life is so predictable, it would have been a waste of psychic power.

I almost got you a jet action spa . . .

. . . But you can get the same effect in your bathtub with an eggbeater.

I almost got you a really professional looking briefcase . . .

. . . But you'd need a really professional job to use it.

I almost got you a fancy designer overnight bag . . .

. . . But considering your record with the opposite sex, you wouldn't really have much use for it.

I almost got you a parrot . . .

. . . But one birdbrain yakking around the house is enough.

I almost got you a double-wide mobile home . . .

. . . But you live smack in the middle of a tornado belt.

I almost got you a Harley Electra Glide . . .

. . . But leather and bowlegs don't suit your image.

I almost got you 20 belly dancers that jump out of a cake . . .

. . . But some wiseguy gave them the cue in my car on the way over.

I almost got you a wild surprise party . . .

. . . But both of your friends are out of town this weekend.

I almost got you a pair of edible underwear . . .

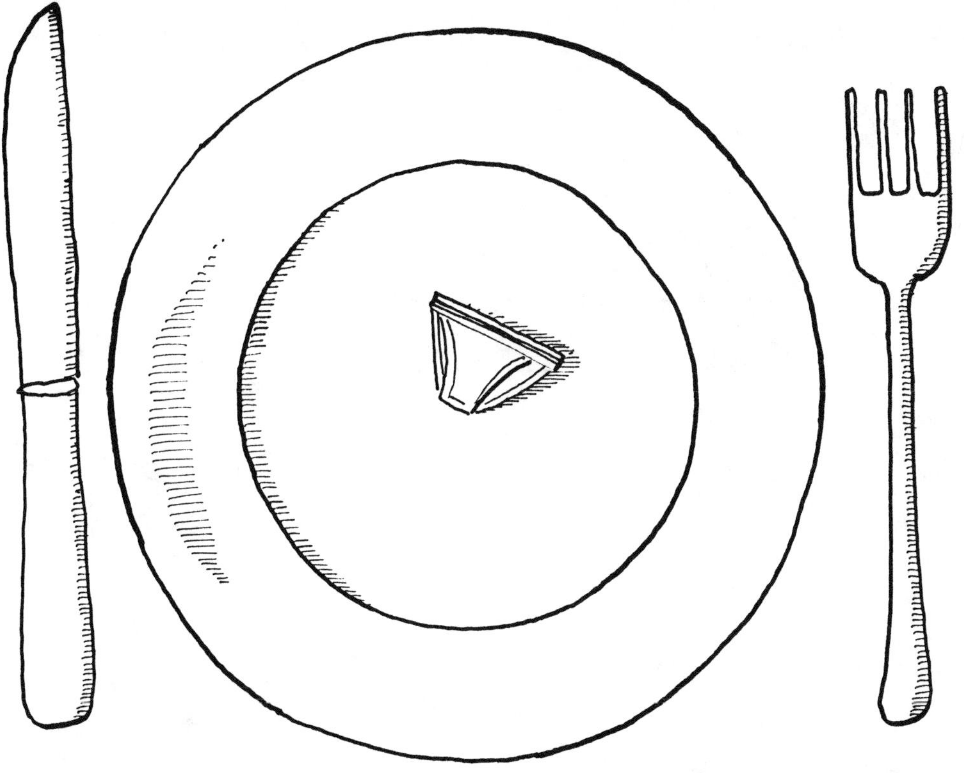

. . . But they don't make a "snack size". Too bad!

I almost got you a 4WD vehicle . . .

. . . But the way you drive, you don't need any extra encouragement to run off the road.

I almost got you a windsurfer . . .

. . . But I can't picture you at the beach without a cooler, lawnchair and TV.

I almost got you a classic Juke Box . . .

. . . But you'd need so many quarters it's impractical.

I almost got you a banjo . . .

. . . But that three hour drive into the foothills for lessons would get old real quick.

I almost got you a lap top computer . . .

. . . But I figured you couldn't use something you can't see over your stomach.

I almost got you a short wave radio with a worldwide range . . .

. . . But you don't even get along with your next-door neighbors, so I didn't bother.

I almost got you an inflatable party doll . . .

. . . But with your luck she'd probably break your heart.

I almost got you a trip to Paris on the Concorde. . .

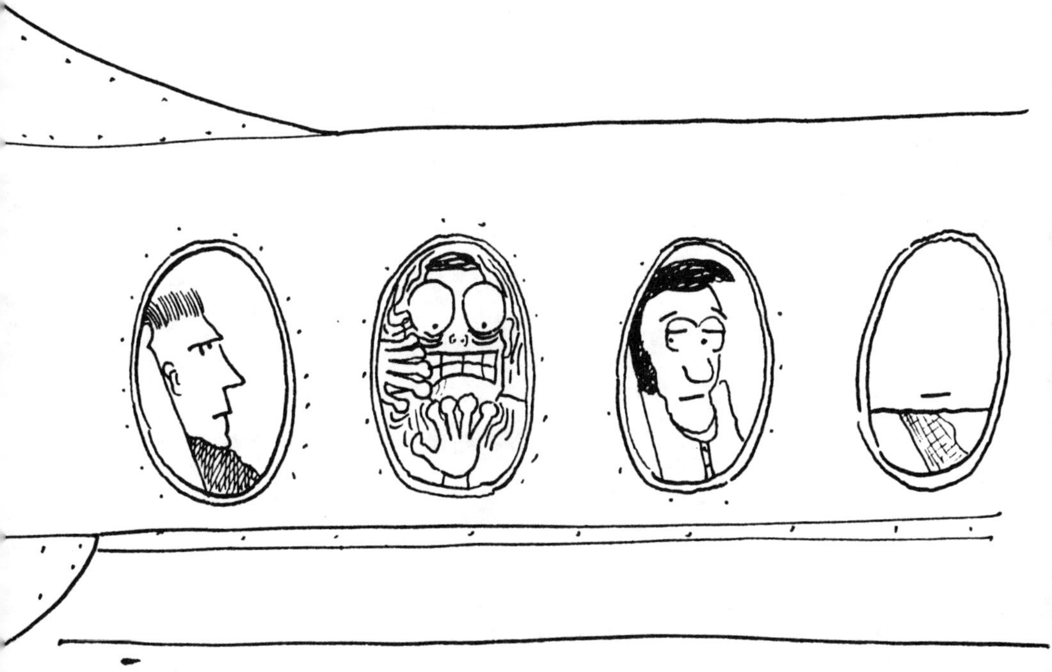

. . . But I know how much you hate to fly.

ORDER FORM

Phone orders by credit card: (800) 345-0096

P.O.Box 37175
Oak Park, MI 48237

ush/Pull/Press

QTY	TITLE	UNIT COST	TOTAL
	The Ultimate Dumb Blonde joke Book	$6.95	
	The Politcally incorrect joke Book	$6.95	
	Gifts I Almost Got You	$7.95	
	The Book of Cold War Nostalgia	$9.95	

es, please send me the books indicated bove. Add $1.25 shipping and handling or the first book and .50 for each dditional book. Add $2.00 to total for ooks shipped to Canada. Overseas ostage to Push/Pull/Press. No cash or .O.D.'s please. Quantity discounts vailable upon request.

Subtotal	
Shipping & Handling	
MI Residents add 4% sales tax	
TOTAL	

END BOOKS TO:

AME: ____

DDRESS: ____

TY: ______________________________ **STATE**_____ **ZIP**__________

ORDER FORM

Push/Pull/Press

Phone orders by credit card: (800) 345-0096

P.O.Box 37175
Oak Park, MI 48237

QTY	TITLE	UNIT COST	TOTAL
	The Ultimate Dumb Blonde joke Book	$6.95	
	The Politcally incorrect joke Book	$6.95	
	Gifts I Almost Got You	$7.95	
	The Book of Cold War Nostalgia	$9.95	

'es, please send me the books indicated .bove. Add $1.25 shipping and handling or the first book and .50 for each .dditional book. Add $2.00 to total for ooks shipped to Canada. Overseas ostage to Push/Pull/Press. No cash or :.O.D.'s please. Quantity discounts vailable upon request.

Subtotal	
Shipping & Handling	
MI Residents add 4% sales tax	
TOTAL	

SEND BOOKS TO:

AME: ______________________________

DDRESS: ______________________________

TY: ______________________ **STATE**_____ **ZIP**__________